Society of Homoeopathic Physicians of Iowa

Proceedings of the Society of Homoeopathic Physicians of Iowa

for 1870 to 1871

Society of Homoeopathic Physicians of Iowa

Proceedings of the Society of Homoeopathic Physicians of Iowa
for 1870 to 1871

ISBN/EAN: 9783337870270

Printed in Europe, USA, Canada, Australia, Japan

Cover: Foto ©Andreas Hilbeck / pixelio.de

More available books at **www.hansebooks.com**

Morning Session.

Pursuant to a call, issued by E. A. GUILBERT, M. D., of Dubuque, inviting the Homeopathic Physicians, practicing in Iowa, to meet on the 31st day of May, 1870, at 10 o'clock, A, M., at Des Moines, a goodly number of them met at the appointed time, at the office of W. H. DICKINSON, M. D.

R. F. BAKER, M. D., of Davenport, moved that Dr. W. H. Dickinson, of Des Moines, act as temporary President, and Dr. C. H. Cogswell, of Clinton, act as temporary Secretary. The motion was carried.

The President upon taking the Chair, ordered the reading of the call for the meeting, and after having made some remarks upon the subject, called upon the members present to give an expression of opinion as to the feasibility of perpetuating the former State Organization, which had been intact for a number of years, or, as to the propriety of organizing a new State Society.

Drs. Connelly, Holt, Jackson, Hunter, Baker, and Seidlitz took active part in the discussion, all being of the opinion that the cause of Homeopathy, in Iowa, would be best served by the organization of a new State Society, and, after a free interchange of opinion, and pleasant, social intercourse, an adjournment until 3 o'clock, P. M., was moved and carried, to give absentees a chance to appear and take part in the deliberations.

Afternoon Session.

At 3 o'clock, the temporary Chairman, Dr. W. H. Dickinson, called the meeting to order.

Upon motion, it was resolved, that the meeting now take steps to organize a State Homeopathic Society; the President to appoint a Committee on permanent organization, and to prepare a Constitution and By-Laws. The following gentlemen were appointed the Committee so ordered:

P. J. CONNELLY, M. D.,	Des Moines.
G. N. SEIDLITZ, M. D.,	Keokuk.
R. F BAKER, M. D.,	Davenport.
L. E. B. HOLT, M. D.,	Marshalltown.
O. T. PALMER, M. D.,	Oskaloosa.

Upon the withdrawal of the Committee, the time of the meeting was occupied by an interchange of views as to the best means to interest all Iowa Physicians, possessing the necessary qualifications for membership, to join the contemplated association.

After the lapse of one hour the Committees eturned, and reported the following Constitution and By-Laws, which, after having been, seriatim, taken up, and in some instances altered, were unanimously adopted.

The report was accepted and the Committee discharged.

Constitution and By-Laws,

OF THE SOCIETY OF

Homeopathic Physicians,

OF IOWA,

ADOPTED MAY 31ST, 1870.

CONSTITUTION.

ARTICLE I.

This Society shall be known as the *"Society of Homeopathic Physicians of Iowa,"* having for an object the advancement of Medical Science, and the dissemination of the law of *"Similia Similibus Curantur."*

ARTICLE II.

The officers of the Society shall consist of a President, two Vice Presidents, a Secretary and Treasurer. At each annual meeting an election, by ballot, shall be held for the above named officers.

There shall also be elected by the Society, in the above manner, at each annual meeting, a Board of Censors, consisting of five members, a majority of whom shall constitute a quorum for the transaction of business.

A majority of the members present shall be necessary for the election of any of the above named officers, and they shall hold their office for the term of one year, or, until others shall have been elected to fill their places.

ARTICLE III.

The duties of the respective officers shall be such as may from time to time be prescribed in the By-Laws.

ARTICLE IV.

The Society shall hold at least one session in each year, at such time and place as the majority of members present at the last annual meeting may determine.

ARTICLE V.

At any meeting of the Society, five members shall constitute a quorum.

ARTICLE VI.

This Constitution may be altered or amended by a two-third vote of the members attending, provided however, that at the meeting previous, notice have been given in writing of such alteration or amendment.

BY-LAWS.

SECTION 1.

Duties of the President :

The President shall preside at all the meetings of the Society, preserve order therein, put all questions, announce the decisions, and appoint the committees not otherwise ordered. Direct the Secretary to call extraordinary meetings upon the written request of members, not less than six in number, giving reasons for such action.

SECTION 2.

Duties of the Vice Presidents :

The Vice Presidents shall perform, in the order of their election, in the absence of the President, all duties appertaining to the office of President.

SECTION 3.

Duties of the Secretary:

The Secretary shall provide a suitable book for records and note therein all the resolutions and proceedings of the Society, also the names of members and the date of their admission. It shall be his duty to file the annual reports of Bureaus and Committees, and any other matter as ordered by the Society; he shall answer all letters addressed to the Society, open and maintain such correspondence as may advance its interest, give notice, at least two weeks before hand, of the meetings of the Society; notify candidates of their election, and the members of the several Bureaus and Committees of their appointment, stating the subjects assigned to them.

SECTION 4.

Duties of the Treasurer:

The Treasurer shall collect all moneys belonging to the Society, make the necessary disbursements, and report annually in writing.

SECTION 5.

Duties of Censors.

The Censors shall carefully and impartially examine into the qualifications of each candidate for membership, in accordance with the standard of qualification laid down by a majority of the Society.

SECTION 6.

Members:

The Society may elect members permanently, according to the standard adopted.

Honorary members may be elected by a two-third vote, but not exceeding two at each annual meeting. Persons so elected shall be entitled to all the privileges of membership, except the right of voting.

SECTION 7.

Fees :

An initiation fee of $3,00 shall be paid by each newly elected member, and in addition thereto an annual fee of $2,00 at each subsequent meeting; a failure to pay after one year, shall subject such delinquent to suspension, until such a time as his arrearages are made up.

SECTION 8.

Papers and Communications.

Original papers and communications read before the Society, become its property, and shall be deposited with the Secretary.

SECTION 9.

Ethics :

The code of Ethics as adopted by the American Institute of Homeopathy shall be held to govern the members of this Society.

SECTION 10.

Bureaus and Committees :

The following Bureaus and Committees shall be annually appointed by the President, consisting of not less than two members, to report in writing at each annual meeting:

1. *Materia Medica and Provings*—Which shall obtain facts relating to Materia Medica : and institute, collect and arrange provings of drugs.

2. *Clinical Experience*—Which shall collect parts relating to clinical medicine.

3. *Obstetrics and Diseases of Women and Children*—

Which shall collect and report facts and observations on the subject pertaining thereto.

4. *Surgery*—Which shall collect all improvements in surgery and surgical means, especially in connection with Homœopathic treatment.

5. *Medical Education*—Which shall act in connection with the committee appointed by the American Institute of Homeopathy.

6. *Anatomy, Physiology and Hygiene*—Which shall report to the Society, the advances made in these departments of medical science.

7. *Medical Electricity*—Which shall report the relation of this branch of science to Homœopathic treatment.

An executive committee, consisting of three, shall be appointed by the President for each successive meeting, which shall arrange the necessary preliminary business of the Society, examine credentials, and do such other work as may be conducive to the efficiency of the session. The Secretary shall be an *ex-officio* chairman ; the other members, if practicable, to reside at the place where the next annual meeting is to be held.

SECTION 11.

Order of Business :

1. Address by the President.

2. Report of Executive Committee.

3. Reading of minutes of previous meeting.

4. Election of permanent and honorary members.

5. Report of Treasurer.

6. Nomination and election of new officers.

7. Report of Committees appointed at the previous meeting.

8

8. Motions, resolutions, &c.
9. Miscellaneous business.
10. Inauguration of new officers.
11 Appointment of new committees by the President.
12. Motions, resolutions, &c.
13. Reading of reports, communications and essays.
14. Miscellaneous business.
15. Unfinished business.
16. Adjournment.

SECTION 12.

These By-Laws may, by a majority vote of those present at any regular meeting, be altered or amended.

The following gentlemen were, in accordance with the report of the Committee, unanimously selected as permanent officers of the Society, for the ensuing year:

PRESIDENT,
W. H. DICKINSON, M. D., Des Moines.
FIRST VICE PRESIDENT,
C. H. COGSWELL, M. D., Clinton.
SECOND VICE PRESIDENT,
P. H. WORLEY. M. D., Davenport.
SECRETARY AND TREASURER,
G. N. SEIDLITZ, M. D., Keokuk.

CENSORS.
G. H. PATCHEN. M. D., Burlington.
L. E. B. HOLT. M. D., Marshalltown.
A. O. HUNTER, M. D., Des Moines.
P. W. POULSON, M. D., Council Bluffs.
E. JACKSON, M. D., Epworth.

Dr. W. H. Dickinson, the President elect, in a few appropriate sentences, returned thanks for the honor conferred upon him by the Society, and he assumed the Chair permanently.

The Secretary read letters from Drs. Worley, of Davenport, and Starr, of Iowa City; also telegrams from Drs. Patchen, of Burlington, and Poulson, of Council Bluffs, regretting their inability to be present, and their sympathy with the movement, and presenting their best wishes for the success of the new Society.

Upon motion, adjourned till 8 o'clock, P. M.

The Society met at 8 o'clock, P. M., the President in the Chair.

On motion of Dr. E. A. Guilbert, of Dubuque, the Secretary read the names of those gentlemen who had signified their intention, either by their presence or by proxy, to become members of the Society.

They were as follows :

AUSTIN, P. A., M. D.,	Muscatine.
BAKER, R. F., M. D.,	Davenport.
BREWER, E., M. D,	Independence.
COGSWELL, C. H, M. D.,	Clinton,
CONNELLY, P. J., M. D,	Des Moines.
DICKINSON, W. H., M. D.,	Des Moines.
DU PUY, N. J., M. D.,	Iowa Falls.
ECKLES, T., M. D.,	Atlantic.
GRAHAM, M., M. D.,	Independence.
GREEN, S. W., M. D.,	Manchester.
GUILBERT, E. A., M. D,	Dubuque.
HILLIS, L., M. D.	Winterset.
HINDMAN, H. R., M. D.,	Marion.
HOLT, L. E. B., M. D.,	Marshalltown.
HUNTER, A. O., M. D.,	Des Moines.
JACKSON, E, M. D.	Epworth.
KING, E. H, M. D.,	Clinton.

10

KING, J. E., M. D.,	Eldora.
LILLIS, W. B., M. D.,	Marion.
LINDER, H., M. D.,	Marshalltown.
McLAUGHLIN, T. C., M. D.	Dubuque.
OLNEY, S. B., M. D.,	Fort Dodge.
PALMER, O. T., M. D.,	Oscaloosa.
PATCHEN, G. H., M. D.,	Burlington.
POULSON, P. W., M. D.,	Council Bluffs.
SEIDLITZ, G. N., M. D.,	Keokuk.
STANLEY, G., M. D.,	Cedar Rapids.
STARR, C., M. D.,	Iowa City.
WAGGONER, G. J., M. D.,	Maquoketa.
WHEELER, B. A., M. D.,	Montana.
WILLIAMS, S. B., M. D.,	Waterloo.
WORLEY, P. H., M. D.,	Davenport.

On motion of Dr. R. F. Baker, of Davenport, the above named gentlemen, whose qualifications were found correct, were declared members of the Institute, and the Secretary was instructed to notify them of that fact, and upon the receipt of the fees required by the By Laws, to place their names upon the roll of members.

The motion was agreed to.

Dr. E. A. Guilbert, of Dubuque, moved the appointment by the President of delegates to the American Institute of Homeopathy, which held its session on the seventh day of June, 1870, at Chicago, Ill., to represent the Society of Homeopathic Physicians of Iowa.

Motion adopted.

The President appointed, in accordance with the foregoing resolution, the following gentlemen as delegates of the American Institute of Homeopathy, to wit:

E. A. GUILBERT, M. D.,	Dubuque.
G. N. SEIDLITZ, M. D.,	Keokuk.
L. E. B. HOLT, M. D.,	Marshalltown.
C. H. COGSWELL, M. D.,	Clinton.

Upon motion of Dr. L. E. B. Holt, of Marshalltown, the Secretary was instructed to notify the general Secretary of the American Institute of Homeopathy of the successful formation of the Society of Homeopathic Physicians of Iowa to furnish him with a list of the officers elect, and to have such certificate countersigned by the President.

The motion prevailed.

Dr. P. J. Connelly, of Des Moines, moved that hereafter at each annual session of the Society a public address be delivered upon some subject relative to the principles of Homeopathy, and that the orator be selected by the Society the year previous.

Motion carried.

Whereupon, Dr. E. A. Guilbert, of Dubuque, was declared the unanimous choice of the Society as Orator of the next meeting.

Keokuk, Lee county, was proposed as the next place of convening the annual meeting of the Society, and the second Wednesday in May, 1871, at 10 o'clock, A. M., as the time. Upon a vote being taken, both propositions were unanimously adopted.

Dr. G. N. Seidlitz, of Keokuk, thanked the members for their selection, and pledged himself to do all in his power to make their visit at Keokuk as agreeable as possible.

The Secretary, upon motion, was authorized to add to the roll of members during the year such applicants as were known to possess the necessary qualifications; he also was ordered to publish the proceedings of the Society in pamphlet form, furnishing each member with three copies, and to procure such stationery, seals, etc., as were required.

The President announced the following Bureaus and Committees to report and present papers at the next annual meeting.

Bureau of Materia Medica and Provings :

L. E. B. HOLT, M. D.,	Marshalltown.
P. W. POULSON, M. D.,	Council Bluffs.
S. B. OLNEY, M D.,	Fort Dodge.
P. A. AUSTIN, M. D.,	Muscatine.

Bureau of Clinical Medicine :

P. H. WORLEY, M. D.,	Davenport.
A. O. HUNTER, M D.,	Des Moines.
W. B. LILLIS, M. D.,	Marion.

Bureau of Obstetrics and Diseases of Women and Children :

E. A. GUILBERT, M. D.,	Dubuque.
G. N. SEIDLITZ, M. D.,	Davenport.
H. R. HINDMAN, M. D.,	Marion.

Bureau of Surgery :

C. H. COGSWELL, M D.,	Clinton.
G. H. PATCHEN, M. D.,	Burlington.
N. J. DU PUY, M. D.,	Iowa Falls.

Bureau of Medical Education :

R. F. BAKER, M. D.,	Davenport.
O. T. PALMER, M. D.,	Oscaloosa.
E. BREWER, M. D.,	Independence.

Bureau of Anatomy, Physiology and Hygiene :

J. C. STARR, M. D.,	Iowa City.
T. ECKLES, M. D.,	Atlantic
J. E. KING, M. D.,	Eldora.

Bureau on Medical Electricity :

P. J. CONNELLY, M. D.,	Des Moines.

13

The members of the Society are especially requested to assist by their personal experience, the Chairman and members of the different Bureaus appointed, so as to enable them to present at the next meeting, full, instructive, and interesting papers on the different subjects assigned to them.

Dr. E. Jackson, of Epworth, moved that the Secretary furnish sister Societies with the record of the proceedings so soon as the same have been printed, and request an exchange of all publications.

The motion was agreed to.

After a few pertinent remarks by the President and Drs. Guilbert, Holt, Connelly and Seidlitz, the motion was carried to finally adjourn to meet again on the second Wednesday in May. 1871, at 10 o'clock. A. M., at Keokuk.

Adjourned.

W. H. DICKINSON, M. D., Pres.

GEO. N. SEIDLITZ, M. D., Sec'y.

www.ingramcontent.com/pod-product-compliance
Lightning Source LLC
Chambersburg PA
CBHW021611270326
41931CB00009B/1437